SUPER-EASY
STEP-BY-STEP
BOOK OF SPECIAL
BREADS

Other Books by Yvonne Young Tarr

The Ten Minute Gourmet Cookbook
The Ten Minute Gourmet Diet Cookbook
101 Desserts to Make You Famous
Love Portions
The New York Times Natural Foods Dieting Book
The Complete Outdoor Cookbook
The New York Times Bread and Soup Cookbook
The Farmhouse Cookbook
Super-Easy Step-by-Step Cheesemaking
Super-Easy Step-by-Step Winemaking
Super-Easy Step-by-Step Sausagemaking
The Up-with-Wholesome, Down-with-Storebought
Book of Recipes and Household Formulas

SUPER-EASY STEP-BY-STEP BOOK OF SPECIAL BREADS

YVONNE YOUNG TARR

Vintage Books
A Division of Random House, Inc.
New York

VINTAGE BOOKS EDITION 1975
First Edition

Copyright © 1975 by Yvonne Young Tarr

All rights reserved under International and
Pan-American Copyright Conventions.
Published in the United States by Random
House, Inc. New York, and simultaneously
in Canada by Random House of Canada
Limited, Toronto.

Manufactured in the United States of America

Library of Congress Cataloging in Publication Data

Tarr, Yvonne Young.
Super-easy step-by-step book of
special breads.

1. Bread I. Title
TX769.T34 641.8′15 75–13374
ISBN 0–394–72010–5

INTRODUCTION

Breadbaking is the most satisfying of all the culinary processes, for in breadbaking we nourish, protect, bring to life living organisms to perform our work for us. All other phases of cooking (with the exception of cheesemaking and yogurt-making) begin with foods that are lifeless before they are cooked.

This extra element, the introduction of the life process, gives breadbaking a certain aura of mystery, a deeply experienced sense of participation that rewards the baker long before the first slice of bread is buttered. For this reason, perhaps, breadbakers tend to be more cultish than, say, jellymakers or picklebriners. Most breadbakers are addicted to the art.

This book takes breadbaking one step beyond the mere production of an honest loaf . . . it offers carefully tested recipes for very special breads. Here is a collection of treasured recipes for water bagels, soft pretzels, raised doughnuts, holiday breads festive with bits of candied fruits and nuts, steamed date and nut bread (the best ever), chocolate bread that tastes like a cake, and even a French bread mix.

These are the recipes that anyone can follow. They contain pared-down instructions impossible to misread. Whether you're a veteran breadbaker looking for new challenges or a novice who wants to be sure of success, these super-easy, step-by-step recipes are for you.

HOW TO MAKE THIS BOOK
WORK FOR YOU

Baking bread is incredibly easy, but you may find it helpful to acquaint yourself with the basic procedures before beginning. These are clearly outlined in the back of the book and are referred to (with page numbers) throughout the text of each recipe. Once you have baked your first bread you will, in all probability, never need to refer to them again.

At the end of the book you will find a few tips on troubleshooting plus a glossary to help you with any hazards or unknown terms you may encounter. It wouldn't hurt to read these few pages before you begin baking.

For the most part, however, each of these recipes is self-explanatory and you needn't do any "homework" before you start.

Contents

THE BREADBAKING PROCESS SIMPLIFIED AND BASIC INGREDIENTS

BREADBAKING SIMPLIFIED

Basically the breadbaking process consists of the following steps:
1 . . . Softening the yeast in tepid water
2 . . . Mixing the basic ingredients
3 . . . Kneading the dough until smooth and elastic
4 . . . Allowing the dough to rise in a warm, draft-free place until doubled in bulk
5 . . . Punching the dough down
6 . . . Allowing the dough to double in bulk a second time (this step is frequently omitted)
7 . . . Shaping the dough into loaves and allowing it to double in bulk in the pan
8 . . . Baking the bread

INGREDIENTS FOR BREADBAKING

Flour: The principal ingredient, which gives bread its basic bulk. The type of flour used — all-purpose, unbleached white, whole wheat, rye, barley, buckwheat, etc., or any combination of these — provides characteristic flavor, color, grain and fragrance.

Yeast: A living microscopic plant which causes dough to rise high and light. Packaged dry active yeast is the easiest type to use, since it remains fresh for long periods of time if refrigerated. Compressed yeast may be used, but its storage life is short even when refrigerated.

Milk: The liquid generally used to moisten the dry ingredients in the dough. Bread recipes most frequently call for whole milk, instant nonfat dry milk in reconstituted form, or evaporated milk.

Water: Usually used to soften yeast and occasionally used as the primary liquid in some types of bread.

Fruit Juices: Used to add flavor and characteristic taste to some specialty breads.

Sugar, Honey and **Molasses:** The sweeteners most frequently used in preparing bread dough.

Shortening: Enriches the dough and imparts tenderness and flavor to the finished loaf. Butter is by far the best type of shortening, but margarine, lard or vegetable oils are also appropriate.

Eggs: Not an integral part of all breads. When used, however, they impart a delicate texture to the finished loaf.

Salt: Regulates yeast activity and is therefore an important breadbaking ingredient.

Nuts, Fruit, Herbs, Spices, etc.: Occasionally called for in particular recipes.

EQUIPMENT

BASIC EQUIPMENT LIST

Mixing bowls
Mixing spoons
Measuring cups and spoons
Wooden pastry board
Baking pans or sheets

DESCRIPTION OF BREADBAKING EQUIPMENT

Mixing Bowls: For mixing ingredients or for holding the kneaded dough while it doubles in bulk. Ceramic bowls are best.

Mixing Spoons: A wooden spoon is preferable, but any large spoon will do.

Measuring Cups and Spoons: Used to ensure accurate measurements.

Pastry Board: Used when rolling out or kneading the dough.

Rolling Pin: Used for rolling out dough prior to shaping loaves.

Baking Pans: Rectangular aluminum pans of standard size ($4\frac{1}{2}''\times 8\frac{1}{2}''$ or $5\frac{1}{4}''\times 9\frac{1}{4}''$) are best. To clean after use, scrape out residue and wipe well. This eventually imparts a patina that makes bread stick less. If aluminum pans are unavailable, ovenproof glass baking dishes or, in some instances, baking sheets may be used.

RECIPES

WATER BAGELS

Yes, it is possible to home-bake bagels even more delectable than the bakery or delicatessen variety. All you need is a good recipe and a little patience.

(Yield: 1 dozen)

INGREDIENTS FOR DOUGH

4 to 5 Cups all-purpose flour
1 Package dry active yeast
3 Tablespoons granulated sugar
1 Tablespoon salt
1½ Cups hot water
plus 1 Egg white
1 Tablespoon cold water

EQUIPMENT

All equipment listed in Basic Equipment, List, page 6
plus Electric mixer
Baking sheets
Large, heavy skillet
Rolling pin

STEP ONE
MIXING THE DOUGH

A. In large bowl of electric mixer, combine 1½ cups flour, yeast, sugar and salt.

B. Turn on hot tap water and allow to run until too hot for your hand to stand. Run water a few seconds longer, then measure 1½ cups. Add water to dry ingredients a *little at a time,* mixing thoroughly every time.

C. Use medium speed to beat dough for 3 minutes, scraping bowl occasionally.

D. Add ½ cup flour to dough. Beat at high speed for 2 minutes. Turn off beaters once or twice and scrape bowl.

E. Stir in as much remaining flour as necessary to make a soft dough that does not stick to your fingers.

STEP TWO
KNEADING THE DOUGH

A. Turn out dough onto lightly floured board.

B. Knead for 8 to 10 minutes until smooth and elastic (*see* Why and How to Knead, page 74).

STEP THREE
RISING

A. Place dough in ungreased bowl. Cover and allow to rise for only 30 minutes in warm, draft-free place.

B. Punch dough down (dough will not have doubled in bulk) and turn onto a lightly floured board.

STEP FOUR
SHAPING THE DOUGH

A. Use a rolling pin to roll dough into a 12″ × 10″ rectangle (*see* Shaping the Loaf, page 79).

B. Cut into 12 equal strips 1 inch wide by 10 inches long.

C. Form each strip into a circle, pinching ends tightly together. Arrange on ungreased baking sheets.

STEP FIVE
RISING A SECOND TIME

A. Cover and allow to rise again for 30 minutes in a warm, draft-free place.

STEP SIX
SIMMERING THE DOUGH

A. Pour water to 3½-inch depth in large, heavy skillet. Bring to a boil.

B. Lower heat somewhat and simmer the dough circles, a few at a time, 7 minutes for each batch.

C. As each set is finished, remove from water and drain on towels. Cool for 5 minutes, then set on ungreased baking sheets.

STEP SEVEN
BAKING THE BAGELS

A. Preheat oven to 375 degrees F. Bake for 10 minutes.

B. Beat egg white and water together. Remove bagels from oven and brush with egg mixture.

C. Return bagels to oven and bake for 20 minutes longer, or until golden brown. Cool on wire racks.

PRETZEL ROLLS

These are guaranteed to be the best rolls ever! Soft like a roll, chewy like a pretzel, with crunchy coarse salt as an extra treat.

(Yield: 16 rolls)

INGREDIENTS FOR DOUGH

1 Cup plus 2 tablespoons warm water
1 Package dry active yeast
3½ Tablespoons granulated sugar
1 Teaspoon salt
2½ Tablespoons butter, at room temperature
½ Beaten egg, at room temperature
3½ – 4 Cups all-purpose flour
plus 1 Teaspoon water
Coarse or kosher salt

EQUIPMENT

All equipment listed in Basic Equipment List, page 6
plus Electric mixer
Baking sheets
Rolling pin

STEP ONE
MIXING THE DOUGH

A. Place water in electric mixer bowl. Sprinkle in yeast and stir until dissolved.

B. Add sugar, salt, butter, ½ beaten egg and 1½ cups flour. Beat at medium speed until smooth.

C. Work in as much of the remaining flour as is necessary to make a stiff dough.

D. Cover bowl with aluminum foil. Refrigerate for 4 hours.

STEP TWO
SHAPING THE ROLLS

A. Lightly flour a pastry board and turn the chilled dough onto it.

B. Divide dough in half. Cut each half into 8 pieces.

C. Roll one piece of dough between your hands into a rope about 1½ feet long, then form the dough into the shape of an ordinary pretzel. Work quickly—pretzel dough is springy and will shrink unless shaped without delay. Place finished rolls on a lightly oiled baking sheet.

D. Repeat process until all the dough is formed.

STEP THREE
BAKING THE ROLLS

A. Brush tops of rolls lightly with water. Sprinkle with coarse or kosher salt.

B. Cover with a light cloth and allow to rise in warm, draft-free place for 30 minutes.

C. Bake in 400 degrees F. preheated oven for 15 minutes, or until golden brown.

D. Cool rolls on wire racks.

BREAD DOUGHNUTS

It's great fun to watch these sugared bread doughnuts puff up in the frying pan.

(Yield: about 2 dozen)

INGREDIENTS FOR DOUGH

1 Cup milk
1 Package dry active yeast
2 Tablespoons warm water
1 Egg, at room temperature
¼ Cup granulated sugar
4 Tablespoons melted butter
1 Teaspoon salt
2 Cups sifted all-purpose flour
plus
Oil for deep-frying
Granulated sugar and cinnamon for topping

EQUIPMENT

All equipment listed in Basic Equipment List, page 6
plus
Doughnut cutter
Heavy deep skillet
Rolling pin

STEP ONE
SOFTENING THE YEAST

A. Heat milk to scalding—approximately 180 degrees F. Set aside to cool to lukewarm.

B. Soften yeast in warm water (*see* Softening the Yeast, page 72). Add to lukewarm milk. Stir until yeast dissolves.

STEP TWO
MIXING THE DOUGH

A. Beat egg lightly and add to yeast mixture along with sugar, 2 tablespoons melted butter and salt.

B. Add sifted flour and blend well. Add remaining melted butter and stir until thoroughly incorporated.

STEP THREE
KNEADING THE DOUGH

A. Turn dough onto lightly floured pastry board.

B. Knead for 8 to 10 minutes, or until dough is smooth and shiny (*see* Why and How to Knead, page 74).

STEP FOUR
"DOUBLING IN BULK"

A. Place dough in lightly oiled bowl, turning once to grease top.

B. Cover and set in warm, draft-free place for 1 hour, or until double in bulk (*see* How to "Double in Bulk," page 76).

STEP FIVE
PUNCHING DOWN THE DOUGH

A. Test dough for double in bulk (*see* How to Test for "Double in Bulk," page 77).

B. If finger indentations remain, punch dough down and turn out onto clean pastry board.

STEP SIX
CUTTING THE DOUGHNUTS

A. Use rolling pin to flatten dough into large rectangle ½-inch thick.

B. Cut with doughnut cutter. Dough may also be cut into strips 1 inch wide and 4 to 5 inches long if desired.

C. Arrange on baking sheets in warm, draft-free place for 1 hour or until double in bulk.

STEP SEVEN
FRYING THE DOUGHNUTS

A. Pour cooking oil to depth of 1½ inches in deep heavy skillet. Heat to 370 degrees F.

B. Fry doughnuts a few at a time in hot oil until lightly browned on both sides, turning once.

C. Drain finished doughnuts on paper towels. Sprinkle with sugar and cinnamon while still warm.

CHRISTÖLLEN

This is perhaps the most delicious of holiday breads. Sweet, even-textured, flecked with candied fruits, filled with sugar and cinnamon and prettily iced, this bread certainly deserves its fame.

Note: These breads freeze very well.

(Yield: 2 very large oval loaves)

INGREDIENTS FOR DOUGH

1½ Cups milk
1 Cup butter (2 sticks)
¾ Cup granulated sugar
1¼ Teaspoons salt
2 Packages dry active yeast
¼ Cup lukewarm water
3 Eggs, at room temperature
6½ – 7 Cups all-purpose flour
1 Cup chopped blanched almonds
1 Cup currants
½ Cup chopped candied cherries
½ Cup chopped candied citron
½ Cup chopped candied pineapple
1 Tablespoon candied lemon peel
Grated zest of 1 lemon
2 Teaspoons vanilla extract

INGREDIENTS FOR FILLING

¼ Cup melted butter
½ Cup granulated sugar
2 Teaspoons ground cinnamon

INGREDIENTS FOR GLAZE

1 Cup confectioners' sugar
Milk

EQUIPMENT
All equipment listed in Basic Equipment List, page 6

STEP ONE
SCALDING THE MILK

Heat milk to approximately 180 degrees F. Add butter, sugar and salt. Stir mixture until butter melts. Cool to lukewarm.

STEP TWO
SOFTENING THE YEAST

A. Sprinkle yeast over lukewarm water (*see* Softening the Yeast, page 72). Allow to dissolve.

B. Add softened yeast and 1½ cups flour to lukewarm milk mixture. Stir until well mixed. Set aside in warm, draft-free place for 1 to 1½ hours, until mixture bubbles around the edge of the bowl.

STEP THREE
MIXING THE DOUGH

A. Beat eggs lightly, add vanilla, and stir into yeast mixture. Stir in about 5 cups flour, or enough to make a soft dough that does not stick to your fingers.

B. Turn dough onto lightly floured pastry board.

STEP FOUR
KNEADING THE DOUGH

A. Lightly toss almonds, currants, candied fruits and lemon zest with 1 tablespoon flour. Knead these into dough until well distributed.

B. Continue to knead dough (*see* Why and How to Knead, page 74) for 10 to 12 minutes, or until dough is smooth and elastic.

STEP FIVE
"DOUBLING IN BULK"

A. Place dough in large bowl. Cover lightly and set in warm, draft-free place for 1 to 1½ hours, or until double in bulk (*see* How to "Double in Bulk," page 76).

B. Test for double in bulk (*see* How to Test for "Double in Bulk," page 77). If finger indentations remain, dough is ready to be punched down.

STEP SIX
PUNCHING DOWN THE DOUGH

A. Punch down dough (*see* Punching Down the Dough, page 78). Turn onto pastry board.

B. Divide dough in half. Allow to rest for 10 minutes.

STEP SEVEN
SHAPING THE LOAVES

A. Use your hands to flatten each portion of dough into an oval about ¾-inch thick.

B. Brush entire surface of each oval with melted butter, then sprinkle each with 4 tablespoons sugar and 1 teaspoon cinnamon.

C. Fold ovals in half and pinch edges tightly together with your fingers.

STEP EIGHT
"DOUBLING IN BULK"—SECOND TIME

A. Place loaves on well-oiled baking sheets. Brush tops with melted butter.

B. Set in warm, draft-free place for at least 1 hour, or until double in bulk.

STEP NINE
BAKING THE BREAD

A. Preheat oven to 425 degrees F.

B. Bake loaves for 10 minutes, then reduce heat to 350 degrees F. and continue to bake for 40 minutes, or until breads test done (*see* How to Tell When Loaves Are Done, page 82).

C. Cool on baking sheets for 15 minutes, then remove and place on racks for 30 minutes more.

D. If desired, wrap in aluminum foil and freeze bread at this point.

STEP TEN
ICING THE LOAVES

Prepare glaze by mixing confectioners' sugar with milk to spreading consistency. Brush over cooled loaves. Decorate with whole almonds and candied fruits.

FRUITED BREAD LOAVES

This is a straightforward breadlike bread (as opposed to some of the other more cakey types). The dough is strongly spiced and liberally sprinkled with chopped candied fruits and nuts. Absolutely delicious!

(Yield: 2 loaves)

INGREDIENTS FOR DOUGH
½ Cup chopped dried apricots
½ Cup raisins
½ Cup chopped blanched almonds
¼ Cup chopped candied citron
¼ Cup chopped candied red cherries
¼ Cup chopped candied green cherries
1 Teaspoon grated lemon zest
1 Teaspoon ground cinnamon
½ Teaspoon ground cloves
½ Teaspoon ground nutmeg
2 Tablespoons sherry
1 Cup milk
½ Cup butter
½ Cup granulated sugar
¾ Teaspoon salt
1 Package dry active yeast or 1 cake compressed yeast
¼ Cup lukewarm water
1 Egg
4 – 4½ Cups all-purpose flour

INGREDIENTS FOR BAKING
Melted butter

INGREDIENTS FOR ICING
Confectioners' sugar
Orange juice
2 to 3 Drops almond extract

EQUIPMENT
All equipment listed in Basic Equipment List, page 6

STEP ONE
MIXING THE DOUGH

A. In a small bowl, mix together apricots, almonds, candied fruit, lemon zest and spices, and sprinkle with sherry. Let stand overnight.

B. Next morning, scald milk, remove from heat and add butter, sugar and salt. Cool to lukewarm.

C. Soften yeast in ¼ cup lukewarm water (*see* Softening the Yeast, page 72). Add to milk mixture along with beaten egg.

D. Add flour, 1 cup at a time (follow instructions given in How to Mix Dough, page 73) until the dough is soft but not sticky.

STEP TWO
"DOUBLING IN BULK"

A. Place dough in a well-oiled bowl, turning once to grease top.

B. Cover and set in a warm, draft-free place for 1 hour, or until double in bulk (*see* How to Test for "Double in Bulk," page 77).

STEP THREE
PUNCHING DOWN THE DOUGH

Once the dough has doubled in bulk, it is ready to be punched down (*see* Punching Down the Dough, page 78).

STEP FOUR
KNEADING

A. Knead for 8 minutes according to instructions given in Why and How to Knead, page 74.

B. Knead in the fruit and nut mixture until well distributed throughout the dough.

STEP FIVE
SHAPING THE LOAF

A. Divide dough in half. Shape into 2 rectangular loaves (*see* Shaping the Loaf, page 79).

B. Set loaves into oiled rectangular bread pans. Allow to rise in warm, draft-free place until double in bulk.

C. Brush tops with melted butter.

STEP SIX
BAKING THE BREAD

A. Preheat oven to 400 degrees F.

B. Bake loaves for 10 minutes at 400 degrees F., then reduce heat to 350 degrees F. and bake for 50 minutes, or until breads test done (*see* How to Tell When Loaves Are Done, page 82).

C. Turn breads out onto wire racks to cool. Ice loaves with confectioners' sugar mixed to spreading consistency with fresh orange juice and almond extract.

ALLSPICE BREAD WITH LEMON ICING

This fat round loaf is flavored with allspice, laced with fruit and frosted with lemon icing.

(Yield: 1 loaf)

INGREDIENTS FOR BREAD

2 Packages dry active yeast
¾ Cup tepid water
4 Cups all-purpose flour
1 Cup granulated sugar
1¾ Teaspoons salt
1¼ Teaspoons ground allspice
⅓ Cup butter, at room temperature
¾ Cup milk, scalded and cooled to room temperature
½ Cup dark raisins
½ Cup golden raisins
½ Cup currants
¼ Cup chopped candied orange peel
¼ Cup chopped candied lemon peel

INGREDIENTS FOR ICING

¾ Cup confectioners' sugar
Lemon juice

EQUIPMENT

All equipment in Basic Equipment List, page 6
plus
Electric mixer
Baking sheet

STEP ONE
SOFTENING THE YEAST

A. Sprinkle the yeast over the tepid water (*see* Softening the Yeast, Method One, page 72).

B. Allow mixture to stand for 5 minutes.

STEP TWO
MIXING THE DOUGH

A. Sift flour and set aside 2 cups. Combine remaining flour with sugar, salt and allspice, and sift together in large electric mixer bowl.

B. Stir in softened yeast, butter and milk.

C. Beat for 2 minutes at medium speed.

STEP THREE
"DOUBLING IN BULK"

A. Cover dough and set aside for 40 minutes, or until doubled in bulk (*see* How to "Double in Bulk," page 76).

B. Add 1 cup of the reserved flour to dough. Beat at low speed for 1 minute, or until thoroughly blended. Repeat with second cup of reserved flour.

STEP FOUR
KNEADING THE DOUGH

Turn dough onto lightly floured pastry board. Knead for 10 minutes (*see* Why and How to Knead Dough, page 74), then knead in the raisins, currants, and candied orange and lemon peel until well distributed.

STEP FIVE
"DOUBLING IN BULK" – SECOND TIME

A. Place dough in well-oiled bowl. Turn once to grease top.

B. Cover and set in a warm, draft-free place for 1¾ hours, or until double in bulk.

STEP SIX
PUNCHING DOWN THE DOUGH

A. Test for double in bulk (*see* How to Test for "Double in Bulk," page 77).

B. Punch the dough down (*see* Punching Down the Dough, page 78).

STEP SEVEN
SHAPING THE LOAF

Turn dough onto lightly floured pastry board and pat into a round loaf.

STEP EIGHT
BAKING THE BREAD

A. Set loaf on oiled baking sheet. Cover with a light cloth and set in warm, draft-free place for 1½ to 2 hours, or until double in bulk.

B. Bake in preheated 350 degrees F. oven for 45 minutes, or until bread tests done (*see* How to Tell When Loaves Are Done, page 82).

C. Remove from oven. Transfer to wire rack to cool. Ice with confectioners' sugar mixed to spreading consistency with lemon juice.

HUNGARIAN HOLIDAY BREAD

If a rich, pastrylike bread sounds good to you, be sure to try this. Flaky on the outside and filled with sweet, chewy poppy seeds and raisins, it is a superior bread in every way.

(Yield: 2 loaves)

INGREDIENTS FOR DOUGH

¾ Cup lukewarm milk
1 Teaspoon granulated sugar
½ Package dry active yeast or ½ cake compressed yeast
1 Cup butter (2 sticks) at room temperature
⅓ Cup granulated sugar
Grated zest of 1 lemon
½ Teaspoon salt
3¼ Cups all-purpose flour

INGREDIENTS FOR FILLING

1 Cup raisins
½ Cup ground poppy seeds
½ Cup granulated sugar
¼ Cup milk
Grated zest of 1 lemon
1 8-Ounce package cream cheese, at room temperature
⅓ Cup granulated sugar
1 Small egg
½ Teaspoon vanilla extract
plus 1 Egg

EQUIPMENT

All equipment listed in Basic Equipment List, page 6
plus Baking sheet
Rolling pin
Saucepan

STEP ONE
SOFTENING THE YEAST

A. Combine lukewarm milk with 1 teaspoon sugar.

B. Sprinkle yeast over surface (*see* Softening the Yeast, page 72). Set mixture aside in a warm place until it bubbles.

STEP TWO
MIXING THE DOUGH

A. Combine butter, ⅓ cup sugar, lemon zest and salt in large bowl. Mix until well blended.

B. Alternately add flour and yeast mixture a little at a time, stirring well after each addition (*see* How to Mix Dough, page 73).

STEP THREE
KNEADING THE DOUGH

A. Knead for 8 minutes, or until the dough is soft but not sticky, adding more flour if necessary (*see* Why and How to Knead Dough, page 74).

B. Place dough in oiled bowl, turning once to grease top. Cover with a light cloth.

STEP FOUR
"DOUBLING IN BULK"

Set in warm, draft-free place for 1½ to 2 hours, or until dough rises and doubles in bulk (*see* How to Test for "Double in Bulk," page 77).

STEP FIVE
MIXING ADDITIONAL INGREDIENTS

A. While the dough rises, place raisins, poppy seeds, ½ cup sugar, lemon zest and ¼ cup milk in saucepan. Cook over low heat, stirring constantly, until mixture is quite thick.

B. Combine cream cheese, ⅓ cup sugar, small egg and vanilla. Mix until well blended and smooth.

STEP SIX
PUNCHING DOWN THE DOUGH

A. Uncover and test the dough for double in bulk (*see* How to Test for "Double in Bulk," page 77).

B. If finger indentations remain, the dough is ready to be punched down (*see* Punching Down the Dough, page 78).

C. Divide dough in half.

STEP SEVEN
SHAPING THE LOAF

A. Lightly flour a pastry board.

B. Use a rolling pin to roll each half of dough into a rectangle ¼-inch thick.

C. Spread each rectangle with half the raisin and poppy seed mixture. Top each with half the cream cheese mixture.

D. Begin at one end of each rectangle and roll up into a jelly roll shape, sealing the ends under. Place both rolls on an oiled baking sheet. Handle the dough carefully—it is very soft.

STEP EIGHT
BAKING THE BREAD

A. Beat egg lightly and brush over each loaf. Set the loaves in a warm, draft-free place to rise for 40 minutes.

B. Preheat oven to 325 degrees F. Bake for 1 hour and 10 minutes, or until breads are lightly browned on top.

C. Cool on baking sheet. Serve warm or at room temperature.

SCANDINAVIAN CROWN SWEET BREAD

Eat this lovely cardamom-spiced bread toasted, buttered, and sprinkled with sugar and cinnamon.

(Yield: 1 large dome-shaped loaf)

INGREDIENTS

1 Package dry active yeast
1¼ Cups lukewarm water
9–9½ Cups all-purpose flour
½ Cup granulated sugar
½ Cup butter (1 stick), at room temperature
½ Cup brown sugar
1 4-Ounce package cream cheese, at room temperature
4 Eggs, at room temperature
¾ Teaspoon salt
¾ Teaspoon ground cardamom
½ Cup chopped candied citron
12 Candied cherries, cut into slices
Grated zest of 1 lemon

EQUIPMENT

All equipment listed in Basic Equipment List, page 6
plus
3- to 4-Quart ovenproof aluminum saucepan
Aluminum foil

STEP ONE
SOFTENING THE YEAST

A. Sprinkle yeast over warm water in a large bowl (*see* Softening the Yeast, page 72).

B. Stir 4½ cups flour and ½ cup granulated sugar into softened yeast. Set aside for 40 minutes in a warm, draft-free place to rise.

STEP TWO
MIXING THE DOUGH

A. Cream butter together with brown sugar and cream cheese. When well blended, beat eggs lightly and add to mixture.

B. Combine creamed mixture with yeast mixture. Add salt, cardamom, candied fruits and lemon zest.

C. Add as much remaining flour as is necessary to produce a soft dough that does not stick to your fingers (*see* How to Mix Dough, page 73).

STEP THREE
KNEADING THE DOUGH

Turn out dough onto lightly floured pastry board. Knead for 8 to 10 minutes, or until the dough is smooth and elastic (*see* Why and How to Knead, page 74).

STEP FOUR
"DOUBLING IN BULK"

A. Set dough in a well-oiled bowl, turning once to grease top.

B. Cover and set in warm, draft-free place for 1¼ hours, or until dough doubles in bulk (*see* How to Test for "Double in Bulk," page 77).

STEP FIVE
PUNCHING DOWN THE DOUGH

If finger indentations remain after dough has doubled in bulk, it is ready to be punched down (*see* Punching Down the Dough, page 78).

STEP SIX
SHAPING THE LOAF

A. Use a deep aluminum saucepan, large enough to hold 3 to 4 quarts. Grease well and set the punched-down dough inside.

B. Cover the pan and allow dough to rise in warm, draft-free place until it reaches top of pan.

STEP SEVEN
BAKING THE BREAD

A. Preheat oven to 350 degrees F.

B. Bake for 20 minutes, then raise heat to 375 degrees F. and continue baking for 30 to 40 minutes or until bread tests done (*see* How to Tell When Loaves Are Done, page 82).

C. Cool bread for 15 minutes in the pan, then loosen carefully around edges with sharp knife. Turn bread out of pan. Wrap double thickness of aluminum foil around sides of bread for support while the bread cools on a wire rack.

CHOCOLATE BREAD

If you cannot imagine how chocolate bread might taste, try this for yourself. Don't plan to serve it with meat and potatoes — it's too fluffy and sweet for that.

(Yield: 2 loaves)

INGREDIENTS FOR DOUGH

¼ Cup warm water
1 Package dry active yeast
¾ Cup milk, scalded and cooled to room temperature
2¾ Cups all-purpose flour
1¼ Cups granulated sugar
2 Tablespoons melted butter
½ Cup butter (1 stick), at room temperature
⅔ Cup cocoa
½ Cup hot water
3 Eggs, at room temperature
Scant ½ teaspoon salt
1 Teaspoon baking soda
½ Teaspoon vanilla extract
1 Teaspoon ground cinnamon

INGREDIENTS FOR ICING

(optional)

Confectioners' sugar
Orange juice, rum or brandy
Almond extract

EQUIPMENT

All equipment listed in Basic Equipment List, page 6

plus
Electric mixer

STEP ONE
SOFTENING THE YEAST

A. Place warm water in large bowl of electric mixer. Sprinkle yeast over surface (*see* Softening the Yeast, page 72).

B. Stir until yeast dissolves.

STEP TWO
MIXING THE FIRST INGREDIENTS

A. Stir milk (at room temperature) into softened yeast. Add 1½ cups flour, 2 tablespoons sugar and 2 tablespoons softened butter. Beat mixture until smooth (*see* How to Mix Dough, page 73).

B. Turn the mixture into a ceramic or glass bowl, cover and set in warm, draft-free place for 45 minutes, or until light and bubbly.

STEP THREE
MIXING THE FINAL DOUGH

A. While the yeast mixture rises, cream remaining sugar into butter.

B. Stir cocoa into hot water until smooth, then cool to lukewarm.

C. Beat eggs lightly and add to creamed mixture along with 1¼ cups flour, salt, baking soda, vanilla, cinnamon and cooled cocoa mixture.

D. Using low speed of electric mixer, beat the risen yeast mixture into the chocolate batter.

E. Beat for 6 minutes, scraping sides of bowl from time to time.

STEP FOUR
RISING

A. Divide batter into 2 well-buttered bread pans.

B. Set uncovered in an *unlit* oven to rise for 1 hour.

C. With pans still in oven, turn the heat to 350 degrees F.

STEP FIVE
BAKING THE LOAVES

A. Bake for 55 minutes, or until breads spring back when centers are pressed lightly.

B. Place pans on wire racks and cool for 10 minutes. Turn loaves out of pans and cool on rack to room temperature.

STEP SIX
ICING THE LOAVES

If desired, mix confectioners' sugar and orange juice (or liquor like rum or brandy) to spreading consistency. Flavor with 3 drops almond flavoring. Spread on tops of cooled loaves.

STEAMED DATE AND NUT BREAD

The perfect bread for lunch or tea . . . moist and crumbly date and nut bread steamed in a can.
(Yield: 4 to 6 breads)

INGREDIENTS FOR BREAD

¼ Cup dark rum
¾ Cup water
½ Pound pitted dates
½ Cup granulated sugar
½ Cup vegetable shortening
2 Eggs, at room temperature
½ Cup unsulfured molasses
1 Teaspoon baking soda
1 Teaspoon baking powder
½ Teaspoon salt
½ Teaspoon ground cinnamon
½ Teaspoon ground nutmeg
¼ Teaspoon ground cloves
¼ Teaspoon ground ginger
2 Cups all-purpose flour
¾ Cup chopped walnuts

EQUIPMENT

Small saucepan
Mixing bowls
Mixing spoons
Measuring cups and spoons
4 to 6 clean small tin cans, with tops removed
Aluminum foil
Water-bath canner or large pot with rack and cover

STEP ONE
SOFTENING THE DATES

A. Bring rum and water to boil in small saucepan.

B. Pour hot mixture over dates. Allow to stand for 30 minutes.

STEP TWO
MIXING THE BREAD

A. Cream sugar and shortening together. Add eggs and molasses and beat well.

B. Drain dates and reserve liquid. Soften baking soda in reserved liquid and add to creamed mixture.

C. Combine baking powder, salt and spices with flour, sift together, then add to creamed mixture. Blend thoroughly.

D. Chop dates coarsely. Stir dates and nuts into batter.

STEP THREE
PREPARING THE BREAD FOR STEAMING

A. Thoroughly butter the insides of 4 to 6 tin cans. The size of the cans determines the number of breads you will make. Standard vegetable cans are a good size, but you can use anything up to the size of a 1-pound coffee tin.

B. Fill cans ⅔ full with date and nut mixture. Cover each can with several thicknesses of aluminum foil, tied down tightly with string.

STEP FOUR
STEAMING THE BREAD

A. Place tightly covered cans of bread upright on rack in water-bath canner or large pot. If cans seem tippy, prop up with ropes of crushed aluminum foil.

B. Add enough boiling water so that cans are immersed to depth of 1 inch. Cover top of canner or pot with at least two thicknesses of aluminum foil. Secure lid tightly on top.

C. Cook over medium heat for 1½ hours, or until the breads test done.

STEP FIVE
TESTING FOR DONENESS

A. Take care to avoid steam burns as you remove lid and aluminum foil from canner or pot. Untie aluminum foil from one can and lightly press top.

B. If top feels solid to the touch you may presume all breads are done. Should top of bread seem mushy, re-cover can and pot as before and continue steaming until breads test done.

C. Cool, then chill, the breads in the cans. Refrigerate or freeze until needed. Serve plain or with whipped cream cheese.

SOURDOUGH STARTER

Sourdough starter is simply home-grown yeast. Provide a comfortable home of soured milk and flour, and wild yeasts present in the air will do the rest. "Sourdoughs," the Alaskan gold prospectors, were so named because of the bits of sourdough starter they carried from camp to camp to knead up a loaf of fresh yeast bread, no matter how desolate their camping area. You, too, need never have to depend on the supermarket variety of yeast if you concentrate on sourdough breads and their variations. Growing your own starter is a fascinating, inexpensive project that can lead to a lifetime of delicious breads with a distinctive, zesty "sour" taste.

INGREDIENTS FOR STARTER
2 Cups milk
2-¾ Cups all-purpose flour

EQUIPMENT
Mixing bowls
Mixing spoons
Measuring cups and spoons

STEP ONE
SOURING THE MILK

A. Measure 1 cup milk into a large glass or ceramic bowl.

B. Cover with a dishtowel and let stand in a warm place for 2 days.

STEP TWO
ADDING THE FLOUR

Measure 1 cup flour less 2 tablespoons. Stir into the soured milk until flour is well moistened.

STEP THREE
GROWING THE CULTURE

A. Cover and let stand for 4 to 5 days, or until the mixture bubbles up to twice its original bulk.

B. If mold forms and/or there is no bubbling by the 5th day, discard the milk-flour mixture and start over.

STEP FOUR
DOUBLING THE STARTER

A. Stir 1 cup milk and 1 cup flour into starter.

B. Cover with a towel and let stand in a warm place for 3 hours.

STEP FIVE
STORING THE STARTER

A. Refrigerate the starter in a ceramic crock or plastic container (never metal) and cover loosely with plastic wrap.

B. Use, discard or give away half the starter (1 cup) once every month and double the remaining 1-cup starter following directions given in Step Four. This guarantees that the starter will remain fresh, active and alive for years to come.

C. Starter may also be frozen in a plastic container, but in this case it must be defrosted every 5 to 6 months, then doubled (see Step Four) and refrozen.

DILLED SOURDOUGH SANDWICH LOAVES

If you've been looking for a sandwich bread with flavor and texture distinct enough to hold its own under layers of mustard, salami and cheese, this herbed sourdough loaf should end your quest. The dill goes nicely with the slightly sour taste of the bread, and crushed shredded wheat adds crunch and nutrition.

(Yield: 2 loaves)

INGREDIENTS

1 Cup Sourdough Starter (see page 48)
2 Tablespoons molasses
1½ Cups chicken (or beef) broth
1 Cup water
7½ Cups all-purpose flour
¾ Teaspoon baking soda
1 Tablespoon salt
3 Tablespoons vegetable oil
1½ Cups crushed crisp shredded wheat (about 5 biscuits)
2 Tablespoons dried dill

EQUIPMENT

All equipment listed in Basic Equipment List, page 6

STEP ONE
PREPARING SOURDOUGH STARTER

At least 1 week before baking the bread, prepare Sourdough Starter according to directions on page 48.

STEP TWO
MIXING THE STARTER AND FIRST INGREDIENTS

A. The day before you bake the bread, mix sourdough starter, molasses, chicken broth and water.

B. Stir in 3 cups flour, 1 cup at a time. Dough should be very moist.

C. Cover with a cloth and set in a warm, draft-free place to rise overnight.

STEP THREE
MIXING THE FINAL DOUGH

A. Sprinkle the soda over the risen dough and stir in thoroughly.

B. Add salt and oil and stir until oil disappears.

C. Stir in crushed shredded wheat and 1 tablespoon dill.

STEP FOUR
KNEADING

A. Grease 2 loaf pans.

B. Knead the dough in the bowl by punching down 10 times with both fists, then squeezing the dough between your fingers 10 times. Repeat this process for 15 minutes.

C. Form half the dough into a ball and scrape it from your fingers into one of the pans. Repeat the process, placing the second half of the dough in the second pan.

D. Sprinkle ½ tablespoon remaining dill over each loaf and use your fingers to work it into top ½-inch of each bread. Smooth tops of loaves with your fingers.

STEP FIVE
RISING

A. Cover pans of dough with a cloth and place in a warm, draft-free place for 2 hours, or until dough is even with tops of pans.

STEP SIX
BAKING THE LOAVES

Preheat oven to 375 degrees F. and bake for 50 minutes, or until tops of loaves are nicely browned. Remove breads immediately from pans and cool on wire racks for 10 minutes.

SOURDOUGH VEGETABLE AND/OR MEAT BREADS

This sourdough variation can double for both bread and vegetable or can function as a luncheon main meat dish when served hot with melted butter. Just spread the rolled-out dough with vegetable or meat combinations, roll up, let rise and bake. Unusual and delicious.

(Yield: 2 loaves)

INGREDIENTS
1 Cup Sourdough Starter (*see* page 48)
1½ Tablespoons sugar
2 Cups milk
5½ Cups all purpose flour
¾ Teaspoon baking soda
2¼ Teaspoons salt

INGREDIENTS FOR FILLINGS
2 Cups finely chopped zucchini, summer squash, spinach, green pepper, mushrooms, tomato OR 2 cups ground meat
OR any combination of these
1 Cup finely chopped onion or scallion
3 Cloves garlic, crushed
1 Cup grated cheese
Oregano, dill, thyme, sage, etc. to taste
3 Tablespoons butter or oil

EQUIPMENT
All equipment listed in Basic Equipment List, page 6

STEP ONE
PREPARING SOURDOUGH STARTER

At least 1 week before baking the bread, prepare Sourdough Starter (page 48).

STEP TWO
MIXING THE STARTER AND FIRST INGREDIENTS

A. The day before you bake the bread, mix sourdough starter, sugar and milk.

B. Stir in 3½ cups flour, 1 cup at a time. The dough will be fairly moist.

C. Cover with a cloth and set in a warm, draft-free place overnight.

STEP THREE
MIXING THE FINAL DOUGH

A. Sprinkle the soda over the risen dough and mix in thoroughly.

B. Add salt and ½ cup flour. Turn the dough out onto a floured board (*see* Why and How to Knead, page 74).

C. Knead in the remaining flour, ½ cup at a time, until dough is fairly stiff and no longer sticks to the board. (Use a bit more flour if the dough still feels sticky).

D. Continue to knead for 10 minutes.

STEP FOUR
ROLLING OUT AND ADDING THE FILLING

A. To prepare Filling, sauté 2 cups finely chopped vegetables or meat or combinations of these, 1 cup onion or scallion, the garlic and spices in butter or oil. Cool.

B. Divide dough into 2 parts. Roll each piece into a rectangle ½-inch thick. Spread with the cooled filling. Sprinkle with grated cheese and roll up. Pinch seams and ends closed.

STEP FIVE
BAKING THE LOAVES

Arrange on greased baking sheets and bake for 55 minutes in an oven preheated to 375 degrees F. Serve hot with melted butter.

HIGH-RISE RYE BREAD

For those who prefer their rye bread on the light, springy side, here is an excellent orange- and fennel-flavored loaf.
(Yield: 2 loaves)

INGREDIENTS

2 Packages dry active yeast
½ Cup light brown sugar
1 Tablespoon plus ½ teaspoon salt
¼ Cup cooking oil
2 Cups very warm water (about 125 degrees F.)
2½ Cups whole-rye flour
4½ Cups all-purpose white flour
1 Tablespoon fennel seed, lightly crushed
1 Teaspoon grated orange zest

EQUIPMENT

All equipment in Basic Equipment List, page 6
plus Electric mixer
Aluminum foil

STEP ONE
MIXING THE DOUGH

A.Measure yeast, sugar, salt, oil and water into bowl of your electric mixer. Stir.

B.Add rye flour and beat at low speed for 3 minutes.

C.Continue beating while you add 3 cups white flour. Beat for 3 minutes more.

STEP TWO
KNEADING IN THE FLOUR

A. Spread 1 cup white flour on pastry board.

B. Turn dough onto floured board.

C. Knead in flour (*see* Why and How to Knead Dough, page 74), using short springy motions to prevent dough from sticking.

D. Dust hands frequently with remaining flour, pat the top of the dough with your floured hands, then turn dough over. This helps keep dough from sticking to both hands and board.

E. Knead in remaining flour, fennel seed and orange zest in this manner until dough is only slightly sticky and quite bouncy. This should take from 10 to 20 minutes.

STEP THREE
RISING

A. Cut dough in half; shape each piece into an oval the size of a standard loaf pan. Butter the loaf pans heavily and arrange dough in each. Smooth tops of loaves with your fingers if there are any ragged spots.

B. Butter entire top surface of 2 pieces of aluminum foil large enough to cover the top and sides of the baking pans. Arrange foil loosely, butter-side down, over pans and set in refrigerator to rise.

C. Let rise overnight, or until center of dough is even with top of pan. Take care not to move the loaves about while they are rising.

STEP FOUR
BAKING THE BREAD

A. Preheat oven to 375 degrees F. before removing the loaves from the refrigerator.

B. Bake on middle shelf for 1 hour, or until loaves test done (*see* How to Tell When Loaves Are Done, page 82).

C. Remove breads from pans and cool on wire racks.

CRUNCHY HEALTH LOAF

No collection of bread recipes is complete without one really special health-bread formula. This one is more tasty than those sold in health-food stores and much less costly per loaf.

(Yield: 3 loaves)

INGREDIENTS FOR DOUGH

2 Packages dry active yeast
3 Cups warm water
¼ Cup light brown sugar
½ Cup honey
8 Cups whole-wheat flour
¼ Cup vegetable oil
¾ Teaspoon salt
½ Cup sunflower seeds
⅓ Cup coconut, chopped
3 Tablespoons wheat germ
plus Butter

EQUIPMENT

All equipment listed in Basic Equipment List, page 6
plus Electric mixer

STEP ONE
SOFTENING THE YEAST

A. Sprinkle yeast over the water (*see* Softening the Yeast, page 72).

B. Add sugar and honey, stir well, and allow mixture to stand for 10 minutes.

STEP TWO
MIXING THE DOUGH

A. Measure 5 cups flour into large bowl of electric mixer.

B. Add oil, salt and softened yeast mixture. Using low speed, beat for 10 minutes, scraping sides of bowl occasionally.

C. Stir in enough of remaining flour to make a stiff dough.

STEP THREE
KNEADING THE DOUGH

A. Sprinkle 2 tablespoons flour, the sunflower seeds, chopped coconut and wheat germ over pastry board.

B. Turn dough out of bowl and knead for 8 to 10 minutes (*see* Why and How to Knead, page 74), or until dough is elastic. Knead in additional flour if dough seems sticky.

STEP FOUR
"DOUBLING IN BULK"

A. Turn dough into well-oiled bowl, turning once to grease top.

B. Cover and set in warm, draft-free place for about 1 hour, or until double in bulk (*see* How to "Double in Bulk," page 76).

STEP FIVE
PUNCHING DOWN THE DOUGH

If finger indentations remain, the dough is ready to be punched down (*see* Punching Down the Dough, page 78).

STEP SIX
"DOUBLING IN BULK" – SECOND TIME

Cover dough and set in warm, draft-free place for about 1 hour, or until dough doubles in bulk once more.

STEP SEVEN
SHAPING THE LOAVES

A. Turn dough onto lightly floured board and knead for 2 minutes.

B. Divide dough into 3 equal parts. Shape each portion of dough into a loaf (*see* Shaping the Loaf, page 79).

C. Set each loaf into well-oiled loaf pan.

STEP EIGHT
BAKING THE LOAVES

A. Preheat oven to 350 degrees F.

B. Bake for 50 to 60 minutes, or until loaves test done (*see* How to Tell When Loaves Are Done, page 82).

C. Remove from oven and brush lightly with butter. Set on wire racks to cool.

PEASANT'S BLACK BREAD WITH CARAWAY SEEDS AND ONION

The density and moisture of this rich black bread are produced by two unusual ingredients . . . melted chocolate and mashed potatoes.

(Yield: 2 loaves)

INGREDIENTS FOR DOUGH

4½ Cups all-purpose flour
1½ Cups rye flour
½ Cup whole-bran cereal
Scant ½ cup yellow cornmeal
1 Tablespoon salt
1 Package dry active yeast
1 1-Ounce square unsweetened chocolate
2 Tablespoons dark molasses
1½ Teaspoons butter
1¾ Cups water
1 Cup leftover mashed potatoes, at room temperature
1 Large onion, peeled, coarsely chopped
and sautéed in butter
1 Teaspoon caraway seeds

EQUIPMENT

All equipment listed in Basic Equipment List, page 6
plus
Electric mixer
Small saucepan
2 8-Inch cake pans

STEP ONE
MIXING THE DOUGH

A. Mix all-purpose and rye flours together in bowl. Blend thoroughly.

B. Measure 1 cup of combined flours, reserving the rest, and place in large bowl of electric mixer along with cereal, cornmeal, salt and yeast. Mix well.

C. Place chocolate, molasses, butter and water in small saucepan. Stir over low heat until mixture is 120 degrees F. (Chocolate and butter need not be completely melted.)

D. Add liquid mixture to dry ingredients in bowl a little at a time, stirring well after each addition Beat mixture for 3 minutes at medium speed, scraping bowl occasionally.

E. Add ½ cup reserved flour mixture and mashed potatoes. Beat at high speed for several minutes. Turn off beaters once or twice to scrape bowl.

F. Add caraway seeds, sautéed onions and enough of reserved flour mixture to make a soft dough that does not stick to your fingers.

STEP TWO
KNEADING THE DOUGH

A. Turn out dough onto lightly floured pastry board. Cover and let rest for 15 minutes.

B. Knead dough until smooth and elastic, about 15 minutes (*see* Why and How to Knead, page 74).

STEP THREE
"DOUBLING IN BULK"

A. Place dough in well-oiled bowl, turning once to grease the top.

B. Cover and set in warm, draft-free place for 1¼ hours, or until dough rises and doubles in bulk (*see* How to Test for "Double in Bulk," page 77).

STEP FOUR
PUNCHING DOWN THE DOUGH

A. If finger indentations remain, punch dough down (*see* Punching Down the Dough, page 78).

B. Cover dough again and set in warm, draft-free place. Allow to rise for 30 minutes (dough will not be doubled in bulk). Punch down again.

STEP FIVE
SHAPING THE LOAVES

A. Turn out dough onto lightly floured pastry board and divide in half.

B. Shape each half into a round ball. Set each in well-oiled cake pan.

C. Cover and set aside in warm, draft-free place until loaves rise and double in bulk, about 45 minutes to 1 hour.

STEP SIX
BAKING THE BREAD

A. Bake in oven preheated to 350 degrees F. for 40 to 45 minutes, or until breads test done (see How to Tell When Loaves Are Done, page 82).

B. Cool on wire rack.

FRENCH BREAD MIX

Conveniently pre-measuring and pre-mixing crusty French Bread makes for easy preparation on baking day.
(Yield: 2 long loaves or 1 giant oval loaf)

INGREDIENTS FOR BASIC BREAD MIX

8 Cups all-purpose flour
1 Tablespoon salt
2 Packages dry active yeast

ADDITIONAL INGREDIENTS FOR DOUGH

3 Cups warm water
1 Tablespoon melted butter
1½ Cups all-purpose flour

INGREDIENTS FOR BAKING

2 Tablespoons white or yellow cornmeal
1 Egg white
1 Tablespoon cold water

EQUIPMENT

All equipment listed in Basic Equipment List, page 6
plus
Large baking pan or baking sheet

STEP ONE

PREPARING THE BASIC BREAD MIX

A. Place all ingredients for basic bread mix in a large double-thick plastic bag. Shake until well mixed.

B. Secure top tightly. Store in the refrigerator. Once yeast is added, this mix must be used within 4 days.

STEP TWO
MIXING THE DOUGH

A. Shake plastic bag containing basic bread mix well to incorporate ingredients. Transfer ingredients to large bowl.

B. Stir in 3 cups warm, *not hot*, water and the melted butter.

STEP THREE
"DOUBLING IN BULK"

Cover dough and allow to rise in warm, draft-free place for 1½ hours, or until double in bulk (*see* How to "Double in Bulk," page 76).

STEP FOUR
PUNCHING DOWN THE DOUGH

A. Uncover and test dough for double in bulk (*see* How to Test for "Double in Bulk," page 77).

B. If finger indentations remain, punch down the dough (*see* Punching Down the Dough, page 78).

STEP FIVE
KNEADING THE DOUGH

A. Spread 1 cup flour on pastry board.

B. Scoop dough out of bowl and onto pastry board. Sprinkle top of dough with flour and knead in, adding as much flour as is necessary to produce a stiff dough (*see* Why and How to Knead, page 74).

STEP SIX
"DOUBLING IN BULK" — SECOND TIME

A. Cover dough and set in a warm, draft-free place for 1¼ hours, or until double in bulk.

B. Test for double in bulk. If finger indentations remain, punch dough down.

STEP SEVEN
SHAPING THE LOAVES

A. Knead dough for 2 minutes. Roll into 2 long loaves.

B. Butter a large baking sheet and sprinkle with cornmeal. If your oven is large enough to hold them, set loaves side by side. Otherwise, arrange unbaked loaves in two facing semi-circles, the end of one inside the center of the other to form one giant loaf (*see* illustration).

STEP EIGHT
BAKING THE BREAD

A. Slash tops of loaves in 5 or 6 places with sharp knife.

Combine egg white and water and brush bread tops with the mixture.

B. Cover and place in warm, draft-free place for about 25 minutes.

C. Preheat oven to 400 degrees F. Place shallow pan filled with hot water on floor of oven.

D. Bake bread on middle shelf of oven for 50 to 60 minutes, or until golden brown (*see* How to Tell When Breads Are Done, page 82). Serve hot or at room temperature.

THE PROCESS
DESCRIBED

SOFTENING THE YEAST

Yeast is generally softened in a small amount of water before you add it to the basic breadbaking ingredients. Since yeast is a living organism, and should be treated as such, the temperature of the water is crucial. Too high or too low a water temperature may weaken or even destroy yeast.

The two types of yeast call for slightly different water temperatures:

METHOD ONE
(DRY ACTIVE YEAST)

Ideally, water temperature should be 105 degrees F. Pour the required amount of water into a bowl and test by sprinkling a few drops on the inside of your wrist. If the drops feel comfortably warm, sprinkle the yeast over the water and stir until dissolved.

METHOD TWO
(COMPRESSED YEAST)

Pour the amount of water called for in the recipe into a bowl. The water should be lukewarm (about 95 degrees F.). Test temperature by placing a few drops on the inside of your wrist. If the water feels neither warm nor cool, but neutral, add the compressed yeast and stir until dissolved.

When adding softened yeast to the other ingredients, be sure that all ingredients are at room temperature in order not to shock the yeast.

HOW TO MIX DOUGH

Although various types of bread may require different ingredients and methods of preparation, the basic steps in mixing dough are as follows:*

A.Scald the milk (if called for) by heating it to approximately 180 degrees F. Remove from heat and add shortening, sugar and salt. Cool to lukewarm.

B. Soften the yeast for 5 minutes in the required amount of warm water (*see* Softening the Yeast, page 72). Stir until dissolved. Add to the milk mixture. Stir in eggs (if called for). Mix well.

C. Set aside ½ cup of flour to sprinkle over the kneading board. Add the remaining flour, 1 cup at a time, mixing well after each addition. With each cup of flour the dough should become firmer and less sticky. When the dough pulls away in a mass from the sides of the bowl, turn it out of the bowl and begin kneading.

*If your recipe differs from this procedure, *follow your recipe.*

WHY AND HOW TO KNEAD

Kneading—the process in which you vigorously push, pull, fold, and refold the dough for a designated number of minutes—eliminates air bubbles, smoothes the dough, makes it flexible and imparts a fine texture to the finished bread. Proper kneading technique is essential (*see* illustration):

A. Sprinkle pastry board, table or counter top lightly with flour.

B. With floured hands, turn dough out onto the work surface and press firmly into a ball. Place heels of both hands on edge of ball of dough nearest you and press firmly away from you, thus flattening and stretching out dough.

C. With your fingertips, pull up far side of the dough and fold back toward you. Again place the heels of your hands on the near side of the dough and stretch out dough.

D. Rotate the dough clockwise one-quarter turn and again pull the far side toward you with your fingertips, then push away with the heels of your hands. Continue to turn, pull and push the dough for the length of time specified in the recipe. Halfway through kneading time, turn the dough over and continue as before. The dough should become firmer, smoother and more elastic as you proceed.

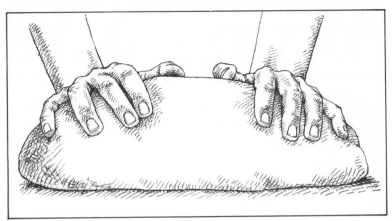

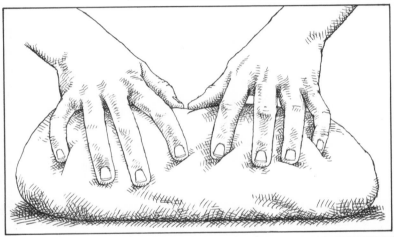

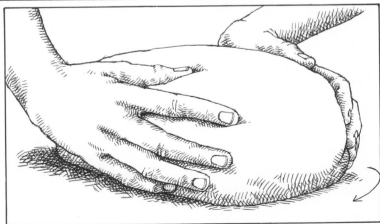

HOW TO
"DOUBLE IN BULK"

Recipes for yeast breads require the dough to rise until it reaches a volume almost double its original size. Breadbakers call this "doubling in bulk." Room temperature, type of flour and amount and type of yeast all help to determine the amount of time needed for the prepared dough to double in bulk. Altitude also plays a part—bread rises much faster at high altitudes.

To help your dough rise properly, follow these instructions:

A. Oil a deep bowl. Set the kneaded dough inside, turning it once to grease the top.

B. Using a dishtowel or other light cloth, cover the bowl lightly and set in a warm, draft-free place for the specified time.

C. Test for doubling in bulk (*see* page 77). Punch down the dough. If your recipe indicates that the dough must double in bulk a second time, recover the bowl lightly and again set it in a warm, draft-free place. Test again at the end of the specified time. Punch down if ready, and turn out for shaping.

HOW TO TEST FOR "DOUBLE IN BULK"

As the dough rises in a warm, draft-free place, it should double in size, or bulk. To determine whether your dough is ready . . .

A. Press two fingers about 1 inch deep into the center of the dough (*see* illustration).

B. If the indentations remain after you withdraw your fingers, the dough is ready to be punched down. If the indentations fill in, re-cover the dough, allow it to stand for another 15 to 20 minutes, and repeat the test.

PUNCHING DOWN THE DOUGH

After the dough has risen and doubled in bulk, it is ready to be punched down.

A. Press your fist firmly into the center of the dough.

B. Fold the edges of the dough toward the center. Press out all bubbles.

C. If your recipe indicates only one rising, shape the loaves after punching down (*see* page 78). If the recipe calls for the dough to rise a second time, turn the dough over, re-cover lightly and allow to double in bulk again. Test, punch down and shape.

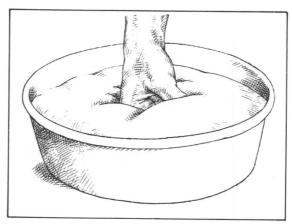

SHAPING THE LOAF

After you have punched it down, the dough is ready to be turned out of the bowl and shaped.

A. Lightly flour pastry board or other work surface. Dust a rolling pin lightly with flour.

B. Turn the dough out of the bowl and set on the pastry board.

C. Use the floured rolling pin to flatten the dough into a rectangle the approximate length of your pan and about ¾-inch thick.

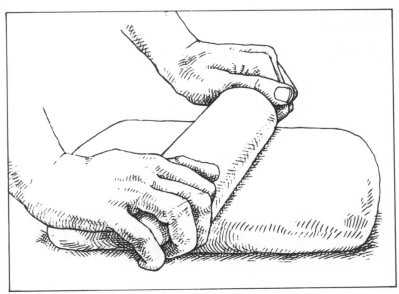

D. Roll the dough into a loaf approximately as long as the pan, as illustrated. Pinch all seams together, turn the ends under, and place the loaf, seam-side down, in a greased loaf pan.

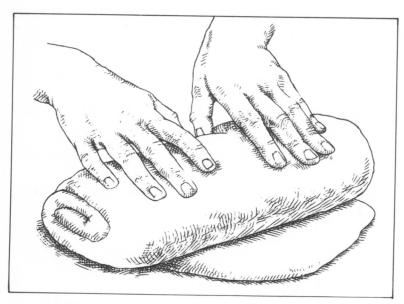

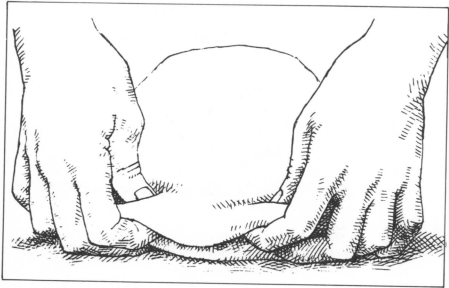

E. If your recipe makes 2 loaves, turn the dough out of the bowl and divide in half by pressing firmly with the side of your hand. Roll out each half as directed above.

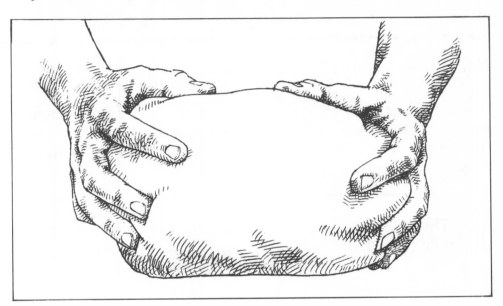

HOW TO TELL WHEN LOAVES ARE DONE

Your bread is perfectly baked when . . .

A. The top of each loaf presents a smooth, shiny, golden-brown appearance. Sides and bottom should also be nicely browned. Pale color indicates that further baking is necessary;

B. The pan resounds with a hollow sound if lightly tapped with a fingernail.

TIPS ON BREADBAKING

ON MIXING INGREDIENTS:

— After scalding milk, add salt, sugar and shortening and allow the mixture to cool to lukewarm before adding the yeast. Excess heat can (and will) destroy the yeast.

— Always soften yeast in warm or lukewarm water, according to the type used. Dissolve thoroughly before adding to the other (lukewarm) ingredients.

— Always have all ingredients for breadbaking at room temperature. Should your recipe call for eggs and should you forget to remove them from the refrigerator in time, cover them with lukewarm water for a few minutes before proceeding.

— Keep in reserve about ½ cup of the flour called for in the recipe. Such factors as the size of an egg or a measurement mistake may produce a stiffer dough than anticipated. Work this reserved flour into the dough at kneading time if necessary.

ON KNEADING:

— Sprinkle the kneading surface with ¼ cup of reserved flour. Turn the dough out onto it. If the dough seems sticky as you begin kneading, add more flour. When the dough no longer sticks to your hands or the board, it is ready to knead. Count kneading time from this point.

— Although dough often cracks or crumbles when kneading begins, continued kneading makes it smooth and elastic.

— Knead vigorously. Dough needs loving but firm handling.

— Knead for at least the amount of time specified in the recipe, and as much longer as necessary to make the dough feel smooth and elastic.

ON DOUBLING IN BULK:

—Be sure your dough has doubled in bulk before proceeding to the next step. If the finished loaf is too dense, it has been baked before it had a chance to rise properly. Conversely, if the finished product is too light, chances are that you allowed it to rise too long. Always test for doubling in bulk before punching down.

TROUBLESHOOTING

—*If dough is too sticky to knead*

. . . sprinkle the pastry board with flour and knead it in, using very quick motions.

—*If bread refuses to rise or doesn't rise on time*

. . . check to make sure you have chosen a warm enough place to set it to rise (especially in winter).

. . . an unlit oven is an ideal place for dough to rise. You may hurry rising by turning your oven on for a *few seconds only,* then turning it off. Set dough inside, and wait.

. . . unless the yeast is too old, most breads rise eventually. Taking extra time to rise will not affect the finished bread.

—*If bread is not brown at the end of the prescribed baking time*

. . . unless your recipe indicates otherwise, leave it in the oven for another 10 or 15 minutes until it does brown. If you wish, you may brush the top with egg yolk before returning bread to the oven for further browning.

—*If bread sticks to pan*

. . . always follow directions given in your recipe which indicate when to turn it out of its pan. Bread which sticks despite this may be loosened by carefully inserting a sharp knife around the edges, or even under one end of the bread. A sharp rap with your hand on the bottom of the pan will also help to pry a stuck loaf loose.

GLOSSARY OF BREADBAKING TERMS

CREAM: To cream generally means to beat butter until light-colored and puffy, and then to beat sugar in gradually until the whole mixture is fluffy.

"DOUBLE IN BULK": When your dough is nearly twice its original size, it has risen sufficiently or "doubled in bulk."

KNEAD: Kneading is the process of "working" the dough with a pushing and pulling manipulation that smooths, blends and elasticizes the dough all at the same time.

PUNCH DOWN: Punching down the dough is done after the dough has doubled in bulk. Push your fist forcefully into the center of the bowl, fold the edges of the dough inward, and press out as many bubbles as possible.

SCALD: To heat liquid to a point short of boiling (about 180 degrees F.).

SOFTENING YEAST: Mixing the yeast in lukewarm liquid to prepare it for the dough.

Yvonne Young Tarr is a veteran cookbook writer. Her books include *The Ten Minute Gourmet Cookbook, The Ten Minute Gourmet Diet Cookbook, 101 Desserts to Make You Famous, Love Portions, The New York Times Natural Foods Dieting Book, The Complete Outdoor Cookbook, The New York Times Bread and Soup Cookbook, The Farmhouse Cookbook* and *The Up-with-Wholesome, Down-with-Storebought Book of Recipes and Household Formulas.* She is married to Sculptor William Tarr. They have two children, Jonathon and Nicolas.